MW00886452

THIS NOTEBOOK BELONGS TO

Made in the USA
Monee, IL
11 August 2021

75506354R00069